D0580024

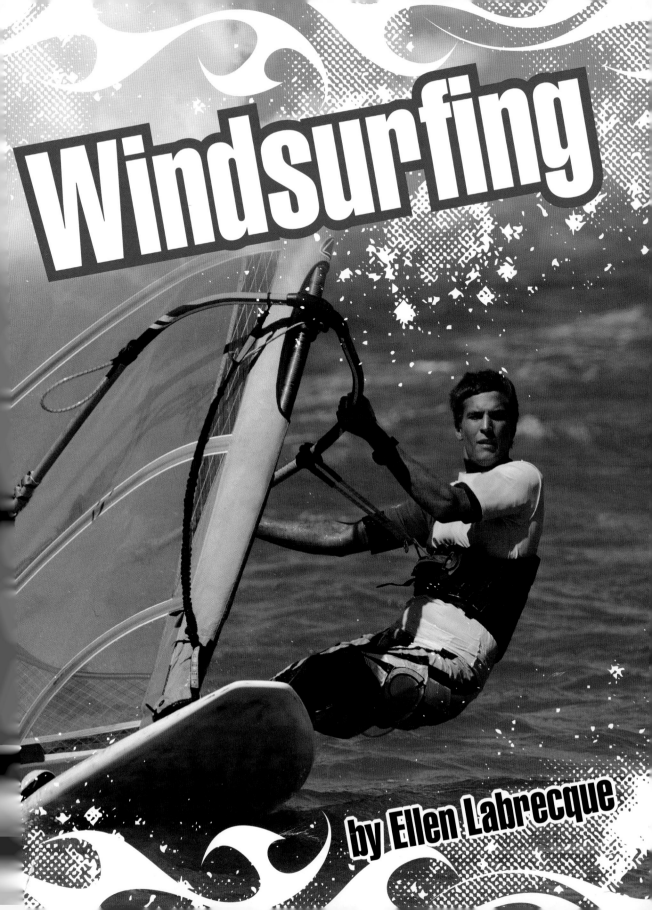

Windsurfing

by Ellen Labrecque

Published by The Child's World®
1980 Lookout Drive
Mankato, MN 56003-1705
800-599-READ
www.childsworld.com

The Child's World®: Mary Berendes, Publishing Director
Shoreline Publishing Group, LLC: James Buckley Jr.,
    Production Director
The Design Lab: Design and production

ISBN: 978-1-60973-188-5
LCCN: 2011928878

Photo credits: Cover: iStock.
Interior: AP/Wide World: 7; John Carter/Professional
Windsurfing Association: 28; dreamstime.com: Dwight
Smith 11, Valeriy Pistryy 16, Tomasz Nieweglowski 19,
Sculpies 28; iStock 8, 20; Red Bull Content Pool:
Eric Aeder 4, Reinhard Muller 23, John Carter 24;
Photos.com: 12, 15.

Printed in the United States of America
Mankato, Minnesota
July, 2011
PA02094

Table of Contents

Jason Polakow challenges enormous waves in Hawaii.

CHAPTER ONE

Gone with the Wind

Jason Polakow's feet are planted on the deck, or top, of his windsurfing board. Polakow, an Australian **native**, is one of the best windsurfers in the world. He is surfing on the waves off Hawaii's North Shore, an awesome spot for windsurfing. Ocean spray hits him in the face as the wind gusts at 25 miles per hour (40 kph). Polakow rides up the wave like it is a skateboard ramp. He flies 20 feet (6 m) up and does a flip in the air. He comes back down and zooms onward. He is ready for the next wave and his next **acrobatic** flip. For this star and millions of others, windsurfing is a real burst of fresh ocean air!

Windsurfing is a sport that combines sailing and surfing. Windsurfers ride on a sailboard, which looks like a surfboard with a pole, or **rig**, attached in the middle. A windsurfing rig includes the sail and the mast to support the sail.

Windsurfing is only 46 years old. S. Newman Darby is the sport's father. In 1965, Darby connected a rig to a board and called his new sport sail boarding. His designs were published in *Popular Science* magazine, but Darby never applied for a **patent** for his invention. In 1970, two men, Hoyle Schweitzer and Jim Drake, did get a patent for the boards. They claimed to be the first to have invented the sailboard. Their sailboard was the same design Darby had created five years earlier. The two men also changed the name of the sport to windsurfing. The argument over who invented the sport continued until the early 1980s. Eventually, all three men were given credit.

A pair of windsurfers sailed across the Atlantic Ocean in 1986 to raise money to help fix the Statue of Liberty.

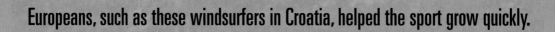

Europeans, such as these windsurfers in Croatia, helped the sport grow quickly.

By the late 1970s, windsurfing was growing by leaps and bounds. The board's design was sold to companies all over the world, including some in France and Holland. The companies could then make millions of windsurfers. Europeans went especially wild for windsurfing. In fact, one in every three households in Europe owned a windsurfing board. By the early 1980s, a professional World Cup Tour was born. In 1984, windsurfing was added to the Olympics in Los Angeles.

Today, there are different windsurfing events all over the world, including speed sailing, course racing, and freestyle. People of all ages are able to try the sport. Many beaches offer windsurfers for rent or provide lessons for beginners.

Whatever kind of windsurfing they do, most people are simply out there for fun and for the love of the ocean.

Driven by the wind, these riders head out for a day on the water.

CHAPTER TWO

Setting Sail

The correct gear is important in windsurfing, especially for beginners. In the 1970s and 1980s, windsurfers sailed on longboards (longer than 3 meters, or 9.84 feet) or shortboards (shorter than 3 meters). These days, most windsurfers use shortboards. Shortboards make it easier for the rider to **plane**. When a windsurfer planes, it skims atop the water like a waterskier, instead of plowing through the waves like a boat. Modern shortboards are made of sturdy foam and weigh from 5 to 7 kilograms (11 to 15.4 pounds) for racing. Beginners use heavier boards of 8 to 15 kilograms (17.6 to 33 pounds).

A windsurfer shows how the board planes, or skims, over the surface.

Windsurfing sails are made of polyester with a mesh covering that does not absorb water. Beginner sails are lighter and easier to **maneuver**. More advanced windsurfers prefer heavier sails that hold up against stronger winds.

Different types of windsurfing use different boards. Freeriding boards are for fun. Formula windsurfing boards are shortboards used for racing. Wave boards and freestyle boards are used for tricks such as jumps, loops, and flips. These boards can be anywhere from 230 to 260 centimeters (7.54 feet to 8.53 feet) in length. Slalom boards are shortboards for going very fast, but some longboards are also used for racing. For instance, racing longboards called Rs:X are used in the Olympics.

A freestyle board is perfect for "getting air" over waves.

Foot straps hold a windsurfer to the board.

Windsurfers use a safety harness to stay attached to the rig. Their feet go in straps on the board. Also, it can get cold on the water, especially in high winds, so riders usually wear wet or dry suits. A helmet is always important for protecting the windsurfer's head.

Once the windsurfer has the right board, sail, and gear, he is ready to hit the ocean. Windsurfing lessons are the first step. Many of the schools are in beach **resort** towns that have hot weather year-round. There are also windsurfing instructional videos on the Internet.

The hardest part of windsurfing is getting started. When you are ready to windsurf, get in the water and push your board into water about waist deep. Get a sense of which way the wind is blowing. Position your board so that when the sail goes up, it will be downwind of the board. Downwind means the same direction as the wind is blowing. Upwind is the direction that goes into or against the wind. Swim or walk to the upwind side and climb on board. Stand up slowly and get your balance. Your knees should be bent and your shoulders back. Pull the sail from the water with the safety rope. Grab the part of the mast called the boom. The boom will help you keep the sail up and steer as well.

Pull the sail up with a hand-over-hand motion.

Turn and Turn Again

The key part of the windsurfing rig is where the mast attaches to the board. This is usually a ball that goes into a hole or socket. This is called a "universal joint." That means it can spin freely in all directions. This lets the windsurfer move the sail any way that is needed to catch the wind or steer.

As you begin to move, you'll learn to steer by tilting the boom. Pushing it to catch more wind in the sail adds speed, pulling it back to "spill" wind helps you turn and slow down. Your teachers will give you more of the fine points, but don't worry if you fall over. Just climb back on and try again!

This rider angles the sail to catch the wind coming from behind him.

CHAPTER THREE

Wind Stars

Robby Naish's nickname is Mr. Windsurfer. He is the face of windsurfing just as Tony Hawk is the face of skateboarding. Naish grew up in Honolulu, Hawaii. He began windsurfing at age 11. He wasn't strong enough to lift the sail up from the water, so an older friend did it for him. But in just a few short years, he was practically a windsurfing expert. He won his first Freestyle World Championship title in 1977 when he was just 13. Since then, he has won 24 world championship titles and was inducted into the Professional Windsurfers Hall of Fame in 2002. Although he is retired today, he still wrestles the ocean every day.

"I love nothing more than a good day of windsurfing," he says. "I can still make that water boil."

Robby Naish was windsurfing's first world superstar.

Polakow excels in inventing freestyle tricks.

Jason Polakow of Australia is another windsurfing legend. He began his athletic career riding motorbikes. He won the Motocross Junior Championships of Australia when he was 18. He was windsurfing at the same time, and switched to the water full time in 1990, at age 19. That year, he won every windsurfing contest he entered, and finished ranked second in the world. Since then, he has won two Freestyle World Championship titles (1997 and 1998) and has become famous for challenging the world's most **humongous** waves. In fact, he was one of the first windsurfers to tackle Jaws, the name for the famous, fearsome waves off Maui, Hawaii.

"After the end of a big trick on a big wave," Polakow says, "I just want to go and get another one. It is just such a good feeling."

Women windsurfers don't get as much attention as the men. But, Sarah-Quita Offringa of Aruba is one worth watching. Just 19 years old with a high-flying style, she won the Women's World Freestyle Championship in 2008, 2009, and 2010.

"I just really want to show that women can bring it just as good as men," Sarah says.

Windsurfers battle in freestyle events all over the world. Five judges score the competitors based on overall artistic impression and **technical** skill.

Sarah-Quita Offringa won the women's world championship three times.

Top Windsurfing Spots

- Maui, Hawaii: The capital of windsurfing. Temperatures are in the 80s and waves can get up to 20 feet high!
- Tarifa, Spain: The wind capital of Europe. It is on the southernmost tip of Spain where the Mediterranean Sea meets the Atlantic Ocean. This makes the area especially windy.
- Virgin Islands: The inner bays are crowded with beginners. The experts go far out in the Caribbean Sea for the bigger swells.

Awesome waves such as this one draw windsurfers to South Africa.

Windsurfers also compete in full-on races. One of the biggest speed competitions is called the Down Wind Dash. The race takes place in February each year off the Western Cape **Province** of South Africa. More than 300 windsurfers from around the world sail in a 20-kilometer race.

Whether doing tricks on the waves, planing on top of the water for speed, or sailing just for fun, windsurfing is a rippin' sport for everybody. So pull up the sail, find your balance, and let the wind be your guide. It's time to get moving!

Glossary

acrobatic—performing tricks that require skill and the power to move quickly and easily

humungous —extremely enormous

maneuver—to move in a way that steers or directs

native—person born in the country where he dwells

patent—the legal right to call an invention your own. It gives you full credit and responsibility for it.

plane—riding on top of the water

province—a territory or division of a country

resort—a place where people go to relax

rig—the name of the mast, boom, and sail of a windsurfer

technical—having to do with the specific gear or techniques of a sport

Find Out More

BOOKS

Start Windsurfing Right!
By James Coutts. Portsmouth, RI: U.S. Sailing Association, 2001.
One of the best guides for beginner windsurfers.

Windsurfing
By Peter Hart. Ramsbury, Marlborough, Wiltshire, UK: Crowood Press, 2004.
This book is packed full of amazing photographs of the sport.

WEB SITES

For links to learn more about extreme sports: **childsworld.com/links**

Note to Parents, Teachers, and Librarians: We routinely verify our Web links to make sure they are safe and active sites. So encourage your readers to check them out!

Index

About the Author

Ellen Labrecque is a freelance writer who lives in Pennsylvania with her husband and two kids. She loves writing, running, and covering extreme sports.